HOT SCIENCE

SETI
The Search for
Alien Intelligence

PETER JEDICKE

A+

Published by Smart Apple Media
1980 Lookout Drive, North Mankato, Minnesota, 56003

Produced by Byron Preiss Visual Publications, Inc.
Printed in the United States of America

Edited by Howard Zimmerman
Associate editor: Janine Rosado
Design templates by Tom Draper Studio
Cover and interior layouts by Gilda Hannah
Cover art: Pat Rawlings. Courtesy NASA

Library of Congress Cataloging-in-Publication Data

Jedicke, Peter.
SETI: the search for alien intelligence / by Peter Jedicke.
p. cm. — (Hot science)
Summary: Describes the work of the SETI (Search for Extraterrestrial Intelligence) Project, which is committed to finding some signs of intelligent life beyond Earth.
ISBN 1-58340-369-8

1. Life on other planets—Juvenile literature. 2. Interstellar communication—Juvenile literature. [1. Life on other planets. 2. Interstellar communication.] I. Title. II. Series.
QB54.J43 2003   576.8'39—dc21   2003042415

First Edition

9 8 7 6 5 4 3 2 1

CONTENTS

The Human Adventure

INTRODUCTION

There are footprints on the Moon. They are dry, colorless footprints because moondust, fine and powdery, is like that. They were made by sturdy boots with unique parallel treads. A footprint seems like such a simple thing, but think of it—human footprints on the Moon! The grand adventure of life has left its earthly cradle and is off and running in the Universe. Former United States President Richard Nixon told the first astronauts to set foot on the Moon that "the heavens have become a part of man's world" less than a century after novelist Jules Verne called taking possession of the Moon "the grandest idea that ever set a human brain on fire."

Those footprints left by astronauts, along with equipment they discarded, are likely the only signs of life on the Moon. But there is a mighty vast Universe out there, and the question of whether life will be found in it elsewhere has also put a spark in the human brain. Scientists are actively searching for signs of such life, studying what it might be like and whether it might be intelligent. Today the search for alien intelligence is speculative. But Canadian astronomer Terence Dickinson suggests that it is "reasonable to assume that long ago, advanced extraterrestrials discovered that life exists on Earth."

Now it is our turn to discover them. Perhaps one day soon, on some distant world, we will find footprints made not by us, but left behind by another space-faring civilization. Perhaps we will come face-to-face with

Apollo astronaut Neil Armstrong's bootprint on the lunar surface. Because the Moon has no atmosphere, the print will remain there unchanged.

those space travelers, come to know them, and work together with them. What would that be like? Or perhaps they will be long gone, their own world grown cold a billion years in the past.

SETI: The Search for Alien Intelligence will explore this quest for other advanced beings—a quest for what life is and what forms it might take elsewhere in this far-flung and majestic Universe.

Apollo astronauts left various pieces of equipment on the Moon, including an American flag. These, plus their footprints, are the only signs of life on the Moon.

Visionary Astronaut

"Discovery begins when you see something you don't expect. Then you stop and say, 'Wait a minute, what is this?' "

(Gene Shoemaker, Apollo program lunar geologist, talking about the possibility of finding answers to age-old questions by examining rocks returned from the Moon.)

What Is SETI?

CHAPTER ONE

Seti stands for "Search for Extraterrestrial Intelligence." (It is pronounced "SET-ee.") The search is an attempt to locate alien civilizations anywhere in the Universe. People have always enjoyed the company of other humans, from the earliest tribes on the savannahs of Africa to the busiest executives in the concrete canyons of Chicago. A search for other, non-earthly beings—whether they are like us or completely different—involves not just one area of science. Even philosophy and psychology have become part of SETI. SETI includes anything that can help in the search, and government scientists, university professors, private corporations, or even individuals at home can participate in SETI research.

The search begins with a basic understanding of life. Intelligent beings anywhere would have to be living things. What is alive, and what is not, may be obvious in a forest or a swimming pool, but scientists must make the distinction clearly if they want to avoid confusion as they search the Universe. The word "life" refers to any complex system of atoms and molecules that actively resists decay. Life as we understand it uses chemical reactions for survival, growth, interaction, reproduction, and dominance over its environment. This definition is somewhat flexible. For instance, it is possible to imagine that electronic circuits might do the job of chemical reactions if robotic computers continue to improve. Or perhaps we will soon revise our view that life must dominate its environment and, instead, think of life as being in harmony with the other living things around it.

If we are going to find other worlds that harbor advanced beings, scientists need to know what signs of life to look for. Would life function the same way for beings on an alien world? Could chemical reactions work there that are different from the ones we associate with life on Earth? Is water always one of the necessary chemicals? Scientists are studying these questions and many others today. Researchers are scouring Earth—the land, the sea, and even the air—for evidence that will expand our knowledge, and they are peering into the sky for hints out there.

For almost half a century, we have been launching space probes and robotic craft. Some of these were designed to look back at Earth and help us gain more knowledge about our home planet. Others have been given missions to seek out alien life, both in our solar system and beyond. When the two *Viking* robot space-craft landed on Mars in 1976, they carried small, automatic chemical and biological laboratories. The machinery took samples of the Martian soil and checked for signs of metabolism, which is the life process that uses energy. On Earth, metabolism always involves carbon dioxide, which is written as CO_2. (This means that it is composed of one carbon atom and two oxygen atoms.) The *Viking* experiments did find evidence that CO_2 was present. But biologists concluded that the soil itself was made of chemicals that produced the CO_2 by a different process, and that there probably was no life within the soil. This is the kind of experiment that might one day reveal signs of alien life on another world.

The *Viking* lander on the surface of Mars. In addition to taking soil samples in search of Martian life, it took the first-ever pictures from the surface of the red planet.

Before their launch, the *Viking* orbiter and lander get final preparation in one of NASA's clean rooms. Spacecraft designed to land on another planet or moon in the solar system must have any dirt or bacteria removed before they are placed aboard their rockets to prevent contaminating samples from other worlds.

Intelligence is a major step beyond basic life. But it is difficult to agree on what intelligence really is. The late science writer Isaac Asimov suggested that intelligence was not a property of individual beings but only of an entire *species* of beings. For a species to be considered intelligent, Asimov wrote, it must be able to develop a complex technology. Asimov concluded that spiders were not intelligent because, even though they build amazing webs, that ability is not a technology that the spiders developed—they build their webs by instinct. Human technology, on the other hand, started with chipped stones and sharpened sticks, and today we have been to the Moon.

If evidence of technology were found across the gulf of outer space, we would be forced to conclude that an intelligent race was out there. So SETI means looking for evidence of technology in any place where it might be found, from footprints on the Moon to sophisticated radio signals from faraway worlds.

What are the chances of success? To estimate the likelihood that intelligent aliens exist in our galaxy and others, American physicist Frank Drake came up with

The *Viking* spacecraft blasts off from Florida in 1975. The robotic *Viking* lander took samples and analyzed them in a search for bacteria and other life-forms. None were found.

an equation in 1961. It is based on the multiplication of fractions. To understand how it works, it is best to apply it to a different example.

Suppose you want to estimate how many students at your school will become astronauts. You begin with the number of students that graduate from your school. Say there are 1,000 students graduating every year. You multiply this number by the fraction of students who will one day graduate from a college or university, since every astronaut is a university graduate. Let's say 60 percent (0.6) will one day go to and graduate from a university. Out of all the university graduates, perhaps 3 out of 10, or 30 percent (0.3), will study science. Of those, perhaps only 11 percent (0.11) will apply to be an astronaut. Let's say NASA recruits new astronauts every five years and will accept one percent of those who apply. (The actual number is far less, of course.) Multiply all these numbers together (1,000 x 0.6 x 0.3 x 0.11 x 5 x 0.01), and your final estimate is that *one* student in your school will become an astronaut. Perhaps it will be you!

Dr. Frank Drake is Chairman of the Board of Trustees of the SETI Institute. In 1960, he conducted the first radio search for signals from intelligent extraterrestrials.

In the Drake equation, the number of stars formed each year in our galaxy is multiplied by fractions that tell, for instance, how many stars have planets, how many planets have water on them, how many might harbor intelligent beings, and how many years an alien civilization lasts. Scientists are still debating each of these fractions, but the smallest number possible for how many civilizations there are in the Universe is one. That would be us. On the other hand, Drake and other scientists have speculated that the answer could be up in the millions, and the Universe could be teeming with alien civilizations.

Spider webs may look like the result of intelligent design but are not an expression of technology. They are not artifacts of intelligence but simply an instinctive output of the spiders.

The Drake Equation

$N = R \times fp \times ne \times fl \times fi \times fc \times L$

N = the current number of advanced, technological civilizations in the Milky Way Galaxy

R = the number of new stars formed in our galaxy each year

fp = the fraction of those stars that have planetary systems

ne = the average number of planets in each such system that can support life

fl = the fraction of such planets on which life actually originates

fi = the fraction of life-sustaining planets on which intelligent life evolves

fc = the fraction of intelligent life-bearing planets on which the intelligent beings develop the means and the desire to communicate over interstellar distances

L = the average lifetime of such technological civilizations, in years

Strange Beings We Already Know

CHAPTER TWO

In the movie *Jurassic Park*, one of its major themes is expressed by the mathematician who says, "Life will find a way." Based on the example of our own planet, the process of life is so flexible that there is almost no situation to which living things cannot adapt. On Earth, everywhere we look, we find life. The paths that life has taken, right here on our planet, are strange and wonderful.

When Earth formed 4.6 billion years ago, conditions were not friendly to life. Over the first billion years or so, the molten rocks and acid oceans settled down. Biologists have uncovered layered rocks that are 3.5 billion years old and contain tiny fossils of once-living cells called "cyanobacteria." The age of these simple creatures means that it took less than a billion years for life to start on Earth. If it was a simple process, the same thing could have happened under similar conditions anywhere in the Universe.

In the 1960s, American biologist Thomas Brock and his colleagues discovered simple microbes—tiny life-forms that require a microscope to be seen—growing in the hot springs at Yellowstone National Park in Wyoming. The temperature was about 160°F (70°C). Brock called this bacteria *Thermus aquaticus*, which means "heat in the water." Most complex life-forms would die at the same temperatures in which these small living things were thriving. Any life-form that can live in conditions that would be deadly to almost all other living things is called an "extremophile," and there are dozens of known varieties.

There are extremophiles that can withstand almost any challenge on Earth. Biologists have found microbes in the ice at Lake Vostok in Antarctica and in the solidly frozen Siberian permafrost. Some microbes can exist in places that are more acidic than normal, or more alkaline (which is the opposite of acidic). Saltiness is also harmful to most life, but there are microbes that survive in salty places such as oil wells and salt flats. Extremophile microbes have even been found living in the Atacama Desert in Chile, and it hasn't rained there in at least 100 years.

Perhaps the most famous extremophiles are the tube worms that live beside cracks and fissures at the bottom of the ocean. They are under tremendous water pressure, have no light, exist in temperatures of more than 220°F (105°C) amid harsh chemicals being spewed out of vents in the ocean floor, yet still they survive. Inside the tube worms there are bacteria, called *Pyrolobus fumarii*, that are so well adapted to the heat that they stop growing at temperatures below 195°F (90°C) because it's too cold for them!

With all this variety of life, it is amazing that the different species on Earth have anything in common at all. Biologists have arranged all of Earth's species into a tree-shaped diagram with three major trunks, called "domains." Every species within a domain is related to all the others in it. But the arrangement of the tree-shaped diagram begins with a common ancestor. Scientists believe that another deep-sea extremophile, the bacterium *Methanopyrus*, has characteristics that make it the great-granddaddy of every other species on Earth. The con-

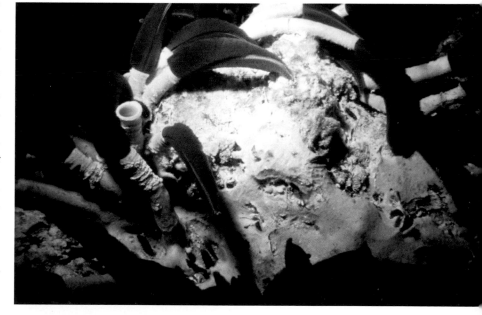

Tube worms grow and flourish in the harshest of earthly environments. Their upper tips, which look like red-and-white flowers, gather nutrients from the water.

The sequence of events from the Big Bang through planetary formation and the appearance of life. From top right, going counter-clockwise: The Big Bang gives rise to matter in the Universe. First-generation stars are born. Their deaths as supernovas create heavier elements. Clouds of hydrogen gas and dust, now with heavier elements as well, come together to form the next generation of stars.

These second-generation stars have planets. The planets are either composed mainly of gases, like Jupiter, or have heavier elements, like the rocky interior and surface of Earth. Comets and meteorites fall to the surface of the rocky planets, bringing with them amino acids and water. These elements combine to form the chemistry of life, including DNA. Single-celled creatures begin to appear, and life is set to evolve on the planets.

Elem

Planetary System Formation

Forming Jupiter-Like Planet

clusion is clear: life started only once on this planet, and all earthly life-forms are therefore related.

The secret ingredient in all life-forms on Earth is a fabulous molecule called "DNA," which stands for "deoxyribonucleic acid." A single DNA molecule contains thousands of atoms, arranged in repeated blocks that are connected in a long, twisted shape called a helix. DNA makes possible the astounding variety of life on Earth. It also carries the information that gives each species its unique identity generation after generation.

But does DNA exist anywhere else in the Universe? Perhaps it does, since DNA is made of the kinds of atoms—carbon, oxygen, hydrogen, nitrogen, phosphorus, and a few others—that astronomers are certain exist all over the Universe. But the same complex structure that makes DNA so good for carrying information also makes it difficult to understand how it first sprung up. The raw materials might be widely available, but perhaps the development of DNA was such a rare and lucky event that it did not happen anywhere else in the Universe. If SETI is successful, we may find out.

It is remotely possible that other life-forms might be based on a different group of chemical reactions. Silicon has been suggested as a replacement for carbon in alien life. Silicon can form four chemical bonds, just as carbon can. This means that a large variety of chemicals can be made of silicon, just as there are so many carbon-based chemicals involved in life. However, there is far more silicon on Earth than carbon, so it is reasonable to think that, if silicon-based life were possible, it would already have formed here. But it hasn't. Another problem with silicon is that the silicon atom is larger than the carbon atom. Because of its size, silicon cannot form what are called "hydrogen bonds," as carbon can. Chemicals that use hydrogen bonds are strong enough to provide structure, but still weak enough to allow those structures to flex. When all factors are considered, carbon always comes out as the best element for building life.

The Three Domains of Life

Eukarya: Includes all larger and complex life-forms, including plants and animals. These organisms have cells containing a nucleus with a cell wall.

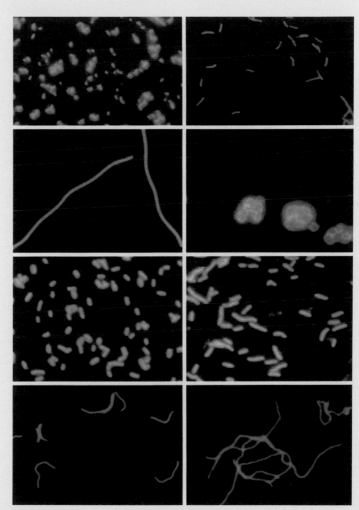

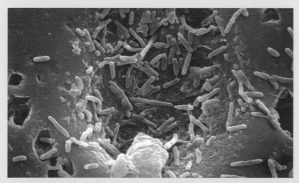

Bacteria: Includes all single-celled life-forms. These cells do not have a nucleus.

Archaea: Includes ancient life-forms that have cells without a nucleus. But the cell walls are not like those of bacteria.

Did Life Come from Space?

CHAPTER THREE

Some science-fiction readers want to believe that life was placed on Earth by an alien civilization long ago, perhaps as some kind of experiment, or perhaps by mistake when they tossed their garbage onto our planet. No scientist takes this idea seriously. However, there is another way that life could have come to Earth from space. It is called "panspermia."

Even in the cold of outer space, ordinary molecules emit weak radio energy in a characteristic way. Astronomers observe this energy with radio telescopes and can positively identify the molecules they find in space. Not long ago, they believed it was impossible for molecules made up of more than a few atoms to exist in outer space. They were surprised when more complex molecules were discovered, and many kinds are now known to be out there. It is possible that the basic molecules of life, such as amino acids, may have formed in the gas clouds of interstellar space. Similar complex molecules have also been found in meteorites that have crashed on Earth.

Two illustrations of Halley's comet. On the right, the comet streaks across the night skies leaving a vaporous trail. On the left is a close-up of the nucleus of the comet. As it approaches the Sun and heats up, its frozen liquids turn to gas and stream out. Crashing comets probably brought water and other molecules important to life to the early Earth.

If amino acids can form in space and arrive on Earth via meteorites, then it is possible that life is not native to our planet, having hitchhiked here instead.

Complex molecules could have attached themselves to tiny dust grains deep in space. And chemical reactions could have taken place if there were enough molecules on an individual dust grain. Because of the chilling cold, such reactions would require millions of years. Nevertheless, scientists such as Nobel Prize-winning chemist Svante Arrhenius a century ago, and Fred Hoyle and Chandra Wickramasinghe in the 1970s, suggested that the most basic life-forms might have evolved in space without ever being near a star or a planet. Panspermia is the idea

Stanley Miller, today, posing with the set-up for the classic electric discharge experiment of the early 1950s, carried out in Harold Urey's laboratory at the University of Chicago.

that these building blocks of life could have fallen to Earth on board a meteorite or a comet. Astronomers peering at comet Hale-Bopp and comet Hyakutake in the 1990s determined that there were many interesting molecules in the vapors released by those comets, such as the complex chemicals methane and ethane.

Max Bernstein and Jason Dworkin, at the NASA Astrobiology Laboratory in California, began to investigate these possibilities in the late 1990s. They simulated the conditions of deep space by using a mixture of ice and naphthalene—the chemical that gives a mothball its distinctive smell. In their experiment, they added in examples of "polycyclic aromatic hydrocarbons" (PAH)—chemicals that have been discovered in outer space by radio astronomers. Then the PAHs in the laboratory were bombarded with ultraviolet radiation similar to the starlight that shines on cold interstellar gas clouds.

What the scientists observed was that the PAH molecules underwent chemical reactions. They were converted by ultraviolet light into chemicals called "quinones." Because quinones are ring-shaped molecules, they resemble some of the important molecules found in living cells. Over a very long time and even in the cold darkness of space, those molecules might combine so that they could be considered to be alive, in a very simple way.

The chemicals brought to Earth by comets and asteroids were important whether they were alive or not. Scientists such as American Christopher Chyba believe that all of the water in the oceans and all the air in the atmosphere of Earth could have come from comets; that Earth had neither water nor air before it cooled. In the 1950s, chemists Harold Urey and Stanley Miller performed a famous experiment in their laboratory at the University of Chicago. In a sealed glass flask, they prepared a mixture of basic chemicals that resembled the raw materials available on the infant planet Earth before the first life processes began. Then they fired electrical charges—sparks—through the flask continuously for hundreds of hours. The electricity represented the lightning that went on and on, perhaps for millions of years, at the dawn of biological time. When Urey and Miller finally opened up their flask, they found that chemical reactions had turned simple molecules into more complicated things, such as amino acids. Amino acids are the building blocks of proteins. And proteins are necessary for the creation of DNA. If this could happen in a concentrated form on a lab bench after only a few weeks, then it was a reasonable guess by the scientists that something similar could have happened over millions of years in nature.

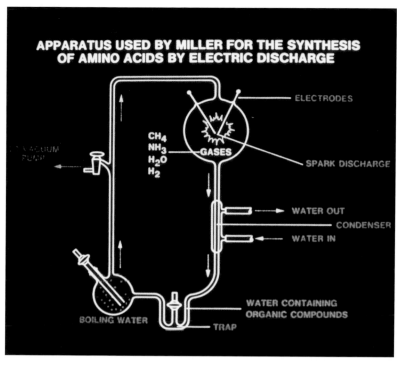

Using electricity and gases that would have been part of the primitive Earth's atmosphere, Stanley Miller was able to create organic molecules in the form of amino acids. This may show the way that life began on Earth.

Strange Meteorites

CHAPTER FOUR

It is possible, then, that the origin of life on Earth is connected somehow with meteorites that fell from space. But meteorites also hit other planets, so if there were some special ingredients aboard meteorites, it is possible that life could be found elsewhere. This theory became famous because of a single meteorite, called ALH84001.

The incredible adventure of ALH84001 started on the planet Mars, which has long been a favorite target for discussions about life existing elsewhere. Mars and Earth—along with the rest of the solar system—were formed out of a giant dust cloud called a solar nebula. Gravity and spinning motion brought the grains of dust together to form pebbles, then rocks, then huge rocks called "planetesimals." The planetesimals crashed into each other during the first billion years of the solar system's history. The gravity of the larger masses kept the bigger colliding rocks together, and the process continued until most of the solar nebula had been converted into the planets and other parts of the solar system we see today. The Sun, made of lighter gases and much heavier than the planetesimals, had already formed as the center of the young solar system.

By 4.6 billion years ago, the big rocks had all been swept up into a few large planets. Internal heat partially melted them and allowed gravity to give them their nearly perfect spherical shapes. And on the surface of Mars, rocks crystallized with a particular mix of small amounts of the chemical elements rubidium, strontium, argon, samarium, and neodymium. Meteorite ALH84001 was one of them. The very slight radioactivity in these elements would forever be proof of the meteorite's Martian origin. But when it first crystallized, it was not a meteorite—it was just a rock on Mars.

A continuing mystery involves water on Mars. Although researchers have not found direct evidence that there is water on Mars right now, there are persistent clues that Mars had plenty of water at some point in its history. Meteorite ALH84001 picked up chemical compounds known as carbonates, sulfates, and hydrates, which scientists are sure can be formed only by water working its way into rock. These compounds formed while the meteorite was still part of Mars.

Meanwhile, tiny glass bubbles also formed on ALH84001. The bubbles were the result of the occasional asteroid crashing into the surface of Mars and setting off shock waves in the rocks. This doesn't mean that ALH84001 was directly hit by a space rock, just that it felt the effects of such a collision. The heat from the impacts melted the glassy material that made up most of ALH84001, and the bubbles formed as the stuff cooled. The bubbles were filled with Martian air and then sealed.

Scientists find meteorites from Mars in the ice fields of Antarctica.

ALH84001 sat on the Martian surface for more than four billion years. If extremophile bacteria formed on Mars at any time, perhaps some of those microscopic life-forms crawled around, or inside of, this small rock.

Then one day, between 12 and 17 million years ago, another asteroid impact hit Mars hard enough to knock the little rock right up off the surface of the planet and out into space.

Meteorite ALH84001, found in Antarctica, may contain ancient, fossilized Martian life-forms.

While there, it was exposed to cosmic rays that don't get through the atmosphere of either Mars or Earth. The cosmic rays caused certain changes to the atomic nuclei in the helium, neon, and argon molecules of ALH84001. These changes are not found in rocks on the surface of a planet but are created by the action of cosmic rays. By examining the rock and discovering its chemical compounds, air bubbles, and the changes to its atoms, scientists were able to figure out where it came from and how it got here.

Careening from one orbit to another, ALH84001 was captured by Earth's gravity a mere 13,000 years ago and brought down through Earth's atmosphere. It landed on the frozen continent of Antarctica, in an ice field known as the Allan Hills. Because this area was part of a glacier system, and because glaciers move,

The Taglish Lake Meteorites

A meteor streaked across the sky over Alaska and northwestern Canada on January 18, 2000. Within days, crumbly black meteorites were picked up from an ice-covered lake. Researchers have found that the meteorites date back to the time when the planets formed. No life-forms were discovered on the Taglish Lake meteorites, but some of the simple chemicals necessary for life *are* there.

ALH84001 was carried along. Over a large area of ice, other meteorites that fell throughout many millennia were also carried to the edge of the glacier. In 1984, geologist Roberta Score went to Antarctica to look for meteorites that had fallen on the glacier. She picked up the little rock from Mars, weighing 4.2 pounds (1.9 kg), and took it with her. (The "ALH" in the meteorite's name stands for "Allan Hills," and the digits "84" tell what year it was recovered.)

Scientists studied many meteorites from Antarctica. Attention focused on ALH84001 when NASA scientists Donald Bogard and Pratt Johnson studied the air in the meteorite's tiny glass bubbles. They recovered the gas without letting it mix with the air in their Houston laboratory. They found that the composition of the gas was absolutely identical to the details of the Martian atmosphere that were reported by the *Viking* robot spacecraft. There is no doubt that ALH84001 was originally a part of Mars.

The most dramatic day in the story of ALH84001 came in 1996. NASA scientist David McKay and his colleagues made a breathtaking announcement:

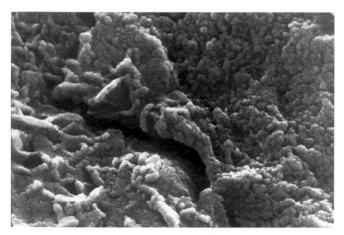

Under the microscope, meteorite **ALH84001** shows forms that are similar to fossils of ancient bacteria found on Earth.

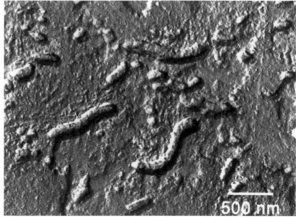

Under higher magnification, the structures found in meteorite **ALH84001** look even more similar to fossils of earthly bacteria. But they could be natural rock formations.

Microscopic shapes that looked like the *fossils of bacteria* had been photographed in a piece of ALH84001. The picture clearly shows what looks like a miniature worm, tiny enough that it would fit between two strands of circuitry etched on a computer chip. Scientists have no way of proving whether the shape really is the fossil of Martian bacteria or just a peculiar microscopic rock formation. As so often happens in the study of life in space, the evidence is always interesting but not conclusive.

Four images of Mars taken in 1997 by *The Hubble Space Telescope.* **Notice the north and south polar caps. Much of the frozen liquid there is water ice. The presence of water means that life may once have existed there.**

Europa and Other Moons of the Solar System

Other than the Apollo astronauts' footprints (and the equipment they left behind), there is probably no sign of life on the Moon. But there are many more moons than planets in the solar system, and some offer fascinating possibilities. The size and chemical components of moons such as Triton, Callisto, and Titan make them candidates for supporting life, but the most interesting is Jupiter's third-largest moon, Europa. Robot spacecraft have photographed Europa and most of the large outer moons as the spacecraft passed by the parent planets. The photographs sent back to Earth show tantalizing details and indicate that these outer moons are not dull and identical. They each have individual characteristics that scientists will spend the next generation studying.

The first fuzzy pictures of Europa were sent back by the *Voyager* spacecraft in 1979. Scientists saw a moon with a strange, white surface featuring zigzagged lines and blotchy patches that definitely did not look like the blasted face of Earth's Moon. Europa is covered with a layer of frozen water that is at least a mile (1.6 km) thick. The zigzag features are ridges of ice at the edges of ice rafts—as big as cities—that grind against each other and get piled up in huge cliffs.

Giant Jupiter and its four largest moons. Centered and nearest the planet in this image is Europa, which has a frozen surface and perhaps an ocean filled with life below it.

An artist's rendition of the *Galileo* spacecraft approaching the planet Jupiter. The robotic craft discovered 11 more moons orbiting Jupiter and sent back images of all the planet's known moons. There are now 39 known moons orbiting the giant planet, one or more of which may harbor some kind of life-forms.

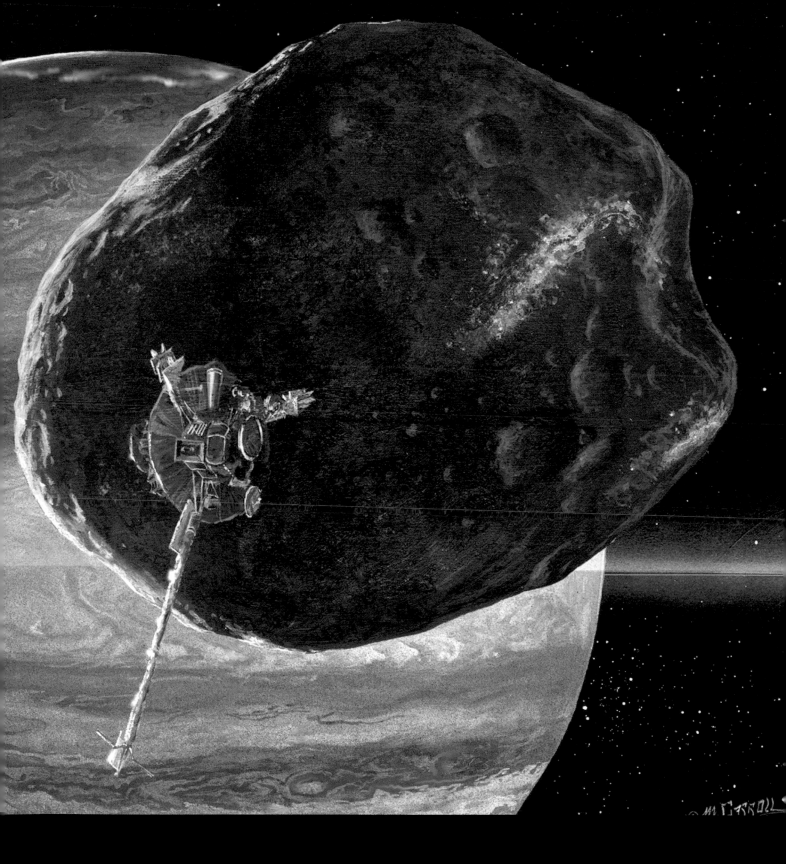

Concept art for NASA's mission to land a robotic spacecraft on Jupiter's moon Europa. The plan calls for the lander to dig through the mile or more of ice covering the moon, then release a robotic submarine to look for signs of life in the oceans beneath the icy surface.

In 2000, astronomer Margaret Kivelson of the University of California at Los Angeles (UCLA) announced that readings from a magnetic sensor aboard the robot spacecraft *Galileo* provided new evidence that there is some kind of ocean below the ice on Europa—probably made of water. Nothing, short of the discovery of life itself, excites biologists like an ocean of water. On Earth, life probably began in the water, and life needs water to survive. Although life is amazingly adaptable and can survive in almost any conditions that can be described, it's hard to imagine life unless water is available.

Why? What makes water so special? No other substance supports complex chemistry like water. Water exists as a liquid in the temperature range that allows many of life's chemical reactions to take place. Water is a simple chemical that consists of two atoms of hydrogen and one of oxygen. Because of the arrangement of the two hydrogen atoms not quite exactly on opposite sides of the oxygen atom, water is an example of a "polar molecule," meaning that it is slightly influenced by electric charge. Other chemicals necessary for life can be dissolved in water, including the oxygen gas that is breathed by fish. Water allows for many chemical reactions that could not occur without it.

Another special property of water is that it expands a little at a temperature just above its freezing point. Therefore, water is most dense and heaviest at about 40°F (4°C), and ice—slightly colder and lighter—floats. As winter sets in, and an earthly lake gradually gets colder, the water

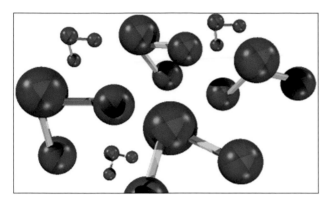

Representation of water molecules. Two smaller atoms of hydrogen (H_2) link to a central atom of oxygen (O) to form a molecule of water (H_2O).

sinks when it reaches its heaviest temperature. Only the water at the surface becomes ice, and it stays there. If ice could sink, a lake would freeze from the bottom up, endangering all life-forms in it.

Astronomers have speculated on whether other chemicals could replace water in a life system elsewhere in the Universe. The possibilities are limited. There are three other molecules that have some of the important properties that water has, even though they do not resemble water. They are methane, ammonia, and hydrogen fluoride. Each of them is liquid over a reasonable range of temperatures, though not so favorable as water. Each is abundant in the Universe, or at least the atoms required to form them are abundant, but not as abundant as hydrogen and oxygen, the components of water. Each supports chemical reactions and dissolves a variety of chemicals, but not as well as water.

Slight variations in the gravitational pull from Europa's parent planet are responsible for warming up the core of this distant moon. (On Io, Jupiter's closest moon, so much heat is generated by the huge planet's gravity that it has created monstrous volcanoes.) There is just enough heat inside Europa to keep water in its liquid form. Volcanoes of cold water may be slowly gushing up there. It is also possible that cracks in the rocks at the bottom of the Europan ocean could have hot vents similar to those at the bottom of Earth's oceans, where tube worms and extremophile bacteria live.

Eventually, scientists will need to send a robot down to the surface of the distant moon. Imagine what a terrific challenge it will be to send a spacecraft halfway across the solar system, land it safely on Europa, and then have it drill through the ice. Once there it will drop a robot submarine that can survive a plunge to the bottom of the Europan ocean and begin to search for life. What a fantastic thrill it would be if the search comes up positive.

Photo of Titan, Saturn's largest moon. It, too, has a frozen surface and may be home to some primitive life-forms.

The Ten Largest Moons of the Solar System

	Name	Parent Planet	Diameter (miles)	Diameter (kilometers)	Surface Gravity (compared to Earth)
1	Ganymede	Jupiter	3,270	5,262	19 percent
2	Titan	Saturn	3,220	5,150	24 percent
3	Callisto	Jupiter	2,996	4,820	17 percent
4	Io	Jupiter	2,264	3,643	17 percent
5	Moon	Earth	2,160	3,475	16 percent
6	Europa	Jupiter	1,950	3,138	14 percent
7	Triton	Neptune	1,682	2,706	18 percent
8	Titania	Uranus	981	1,578	8 percent
9	Rhea	Saturn	951	1,530	6 percent
10	Oberon	Uranus	947	1,523	7 percent

The Clouds of Venus and the Outer Planets

CHAPTER SIX

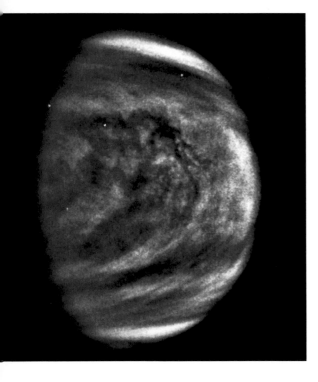

The surface of Venus is forever shrouded with thick clouds. Not being able to see beneath them gave the planet an air of mystery: perhaps there was a planetary ocean and an advanced alien civilization living there, unseen by us.

Seven of the nine planets in the solar system have significant atmospheres. And at least one moon—Saturn's Titan—does as well. These blankets of gases around the planets may be good places for life to exist. The essential chemical elements for life as we know it—carbon, nitrogen, oxygen, and hydrogen—are all found in molecules that are common in the atmospheres. Water vapor and other chemicals that can provide necessary liquids are also abundant there. Sunlight can provide energy from above, and at least a little heat comes up from the molten cores of all the planets. Wind makes movement free, and buoyancy—the ability to float—means that a life-form would not need a very strong skeleton to support itself.

The atmosphere of the planet Venus lets sunlight through, so that the lower layers of the atmosphere and the planet's surface get warm. But then the atmosphere does not release the same amount of energy, in the form of heat, back to space. This is called the "greenhouse effect," and on Venus it has created an inferno. The temperature at the surface is about 850°F (450°C)—hot enough to melt lead. The pressure there is also extreme—about 90 times as heavy as Earth's air. Because of the high heat, the atmosphere howls with winds as fast as 240 miles (380 km) per hour. Near the surface, there is almost no wind.

But the surface of Venus is not visible when someone looks at it through a telescope, just the tops of its clouds. To imagine conditions in the lower atmosphere of Venus, think of a powerful car wash that sprays acid inside of a giant oven. It would be extremely difficult for life to exist there, but the conditions are different high above the surface. At some point, perhaps 30 miles (50 km) up, the temperature is below the boiling point of water. Astronomer Dirk Schulze-Makuch, from the University of Texas at El Paso, has suggested that hydrogen sulphide, sulphur dioxide, and carbonyl sulphide—three acidic chemicals observed in Venus's atmosphere—could be the by-products of microbes floating in the atmosphere. The conditions are no worse than what some extremophiles face on Earth. And bacteria *have* been observed in Earth's atmosphere, carried far across entire continents by the planetary wind known as the jet stream.

Sunlight is much weaker out beyond the orbit of Mars, where the realm of the gas-giant planets begins. All four—Jupiter, Saturn, Uranus, and Neptune—do not have a surface the way that the inner planets do. No spacecraft could land on a gas-giant planet. A ship descending into the atmosphere would find the conditions gradually getting more and more extreme. The temperature and pressure would rise as the atmosphere got thicker and thicker. Eventually, the ship would be crushed.

But, as on Venus, there is a "Goldilocks effect": right in the middle of the atmosphere, not too deep and not too shallow, conditions for life may be just right. Astronomers E. E. Salpeter and the late Carl Sagan proposed that life could have started in the atmospheres of gas giants through processes similar to those that took place in the first billion years of life on Earth. The *Galileo* probe that was

Radar map of the surface of Venus. Now we know that there are no oceans and probably no water at all on the surface of Venus, but there are many active volcanoes.

dropped into Jupiter's atmosphere in 1995 found no evidence of any of these life-forms. Nor was anything of a biological nature observed when comet Shoemaker-Levy 9 crashed into Jupiter the year before. But with such a huge area and depth, it remains possible that life could exist somewhere in Jupiter's atmosphere.

Jupiter is also interesting because similar giant planets have been discovered orbiting other suns besides our own. The chemistry of their atmospheres must be as complicated as the atmosphere of Jupiter. The more planets there are in the Universe like that, the better the chances that life developed on one or more of them.

A fragment of comet Shoemaker-Levy 9 smashes into the southern half of giant Jupiter. These three images are from different points of view. Images 1 and 2 show the impact as the planet revolves left-to-right. Image 3 shows the impact as seen from below the planet's south pole.

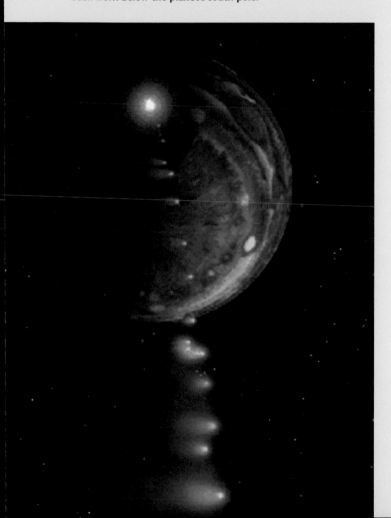

Carl Sagan and E. E. Salpeter whimsically suggested that four kinds of creatures could make up an ecology in the atmosphere of Jupiter.

• "Sinkers": small things like the plankton that live near the surface of Earth's oceans. Like plankton, sinkers would slowly drift downward through the thickening layers and die when they were too far from the source of sunlight. But their offspring would rise back to the surface on warmer currents.

• "Floaters": larger, more complex creatures that would control their level in the atmosphere with flotation bladders. With their mouths open, they would hang in Jupiter's atmosphere like blimps, eating the sinkers that would rain down on them.

• "Hunters": swimming creatures that would control their movement in the air the same way fish get around in water on Earth. They would prey on the floaters.

• "Scavengers": deep down in the atmosphere where the pressures and temperatures would be too high for the other forms of life, these beings would wait for nutrients to fall from the upper levels.

Friends from Light-Years Away

CHAPTER SEVEN

Beginning in 1995, Geoffrey Marcy and other astronomers found giant planets around many other stars in our neighborhood of the Milky Way Galaxy. These planets are larger even than Jupiter, but there is good reason to believe that other planets of all sizes exist. On some of those planets, life might have developed into beings with intelligence similar to our own. What might they be like?

Perhaps we should ask the dolphins. Dolphin brains are about as large as human brains, when compared with the weight of their bodies. The outside layer of their brains, called the cerebral cortex, also shows the same complicated pattern of ridges found in human brains. Along with whales, dolphins have many characteristics that make them different from fishes and other creatures in the ocean. Fossils prove that the ancestors of the dolphins walked on land about 60 million years ago. Their eyes can see both underwater and when they are in the air. Dolphins may even dream when they are asleep.

And yet humans have been able to communicate with dolphins in only the most limited of ways. Dolphins make clicking and whistling noises that imitate sounds they have heard, so they are obviously paying attention. And at least one dolphin researcher has evidence that dolphins can create unique combinations of the whistles they have learned to give their human partners new requests for interaction.

But we have no idea of what dolphins are thinking. Why do they enjoy jumping out of the water? Do they know that their ancestors walked on land? Can they see the stars at night? Does it make them angry that humans dump garbage in the oceans? Still, understanding the dolphin mind is less of a challenge than it would be to understand an alien intelligence. An alien being might have even stranger reasons

for doing things than dolphins. How would we even know what questions to ask?

Suppose there were an alien civilization with technology more advanced than human technology. They would probably be curious about the Universe, as humans are. Perhaps they would want to explore other stars. If they had spaceships that could circle their home planet like the space shuttle can travel around Earth, could they use those ships to travel across the galaxy? The total distance

Dolphins are more intelligent than almost all other earthly animals, but their lack of hands and arms means they cannot build things the way people do. We may find aliens as smart as us somewhere in the galaxy who are also water-bound and therefore lacking in technology.

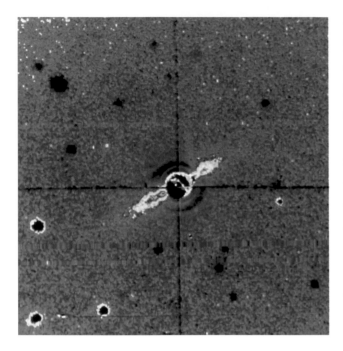

Beta Pictoris, a star in the Milky Way about 50 light-years from Earth. This image shows a planetary nebula around the star, out of which one or more planets will emerge. This photograph was the first direct evidence that our Sun is not the only star to have planets.

traveled by a space shuttle in orbit is a few million miles, but the very nearest star is at least a million times farther than that. The amount of energy that a spaceship from Earth would need to travel to the very nearest star is astounding.

An alien civilization might be able to harness terrific new sources of energy, such as hydrogen fusion. Imagine that they did build a spaceship with far more power than the spaceships humans have built, and they launched it at the fantastic speed of 125,000 miles (200,000 km) per second. It would pass their moon (if they have one) in a few seconds and their sister planets in an hour. But it would still take six years to reach the very nearest star! A trip halfway across the galaxy would require almost 100,000 years and the same to get home.

But wait—there's Albert Einstein's famous theory of relativity. No spaceship can go faster than the speed of light, which is about 186,000 miles (300,000 km) per second. Because of this ultimate speed limit, travelers going extremely fast experience their trip differently than those who stay behind. Time slows down inside of a spacecraft that is traveling at velocities approaching the speed of light. Moving at that speed, a trip halfway across the galaxy would feel like it had taken only a few days to the passengers aboard a spaceship. But on the planet from which the ship left, 200,000 years would have passed. When the explorers returned from the near-light-speed voyage, their "home" would be as alien as any of the worlds they had visited! So interstellar travel is strictly a one-way possibility. Although many humans claim to have seen alien visitors here on Earth, there is no scientific evidence that any aliens have made the effort to visit our solar system.

It's also possible that an alien civilization could build robot spaceships that could survive thousands of years in space. Three of NASA's exploration spacecraft—one *Pioneer* and two *Voyagers*—are slowly on their way into the galaxy and are still sending signals back to Earth. Advanced robot spaceships could be programmed to seek new planets and then build new robots to explore more and more star systems. American physicist Frank Tipler calculates that such robots could visit every star in the entire galaxy in about three million years.

That is a mere eye blink in the history of the Universe. Perhaps Earth has already been visited by such automatic space probes. They could still be here, buried underground, or even on the Moon. When human beings finally discover one of them, it might have stopped working, or perhaps it could be reactivated, as in the famous movie *2001: A Space Odyssey*. Or maybe an alien machine arrived on Earth long ago and taught the dolphins how to whistle.

An artist's concept of an alien world, with two moons and life-forms growing near the edge of a large body of water.

Talking and Listening

CHAPTER EIGHT

Instead of sending spaceships or robots across the tremendous distances of interstellar space, an advanced civilization might want to send messages. Sending a message takes far less energy than sending a spaceship. Using light or radio waves, a signal would travel at the fastest speed of all—the speed of light. But even at lightspeed, waiting for an answer would be a big problem, and it makes anything like a conversation almost impossible.

Sending one-way messages is a reasonable alternative. Human beings are already doing that. When radio transmitters were first invented a century ago, those signals were broadcast in all directions—including out into space. Stronger signals with radio and television programs have been on their way to the stars at the speed of light for 60 years or more. Even though these were not intended as messages from Earth, any alien civilization within range can already eavesdrop on human beings. And the strongest radio waves being sent from Earth are not programs at all, but the powerful pulses of military radar systems. An alien scientist who detects this radio energy will recognize at once that it is not a natural emission from stars or planets, even though there is no message to decode.

The first time human beings deliberately sent a radio message into deep space was in 1973. The giant radio dish at Arecibo, Puerto Rico, was used as the transmitter. The message was a sequence of zeroes and ones, designed to be arranged as a simple drawing. It was aimed at a star cluster known as M13 in the constellation Hercules, 21,000 light-years from Earth. There are many thousands of stars in M13, so perhaps there is a civilization there that will have a radio telescope aimed in our direction when the message finally arrives.

Listening is even easier than sending. The first search for radio signals sent by any extraterrestrial intelligence to Earth began in 1960 and was called Project Ozma. The radio channel that Project Ozma tuned in to listen to was a frequency of 1.42 gigahertz, chosen because it is one of the natural frequencies associated with water molecules in space. Also, radio energy at 1.42 gigahertz penetrates the dark clouds in the Milky Way very well and can therefore be detected far across the galaxy. This frequency is still used, but scientists have now extended the search to many different frequencies as well. In all, more than 60 different radio projects have tried to "hear" the elusive first signal from another civilization in space.

The largest radio telescope in the world is at Arecibo in Puerto Rico. It was built in a natural crater. Part of its job is to listen for radio signals sent by alien civilizations.

The small radio telescope used in Project Ozma was a giant leap forward in SETI. It was the first radio telescope dedicated to listening for intelligent signals from other worlds.

Because funding has not been generous, radio SETI projects are typically small but efficient. Paul Horowitz, of Harvard University, began his search by designing a radio receiver that could tune in 65,536 separate channels. Then he upgraded his receivers to capture more than 8 million channels, and, later, 250 million. Today, Harvard's SETI program covers one billion channels! Radio SETI projects have three goals. First, cover as much of the sky as possible, to have the best chance of catching a signal from an extraterrestrial civilization somewhere. Second, aim the receiver as accurately as possible, to know where the source of a signal is. And third, listen to as many channels as possible, because no one knows what the frequency of an alien signal might be. SETI research also faces the problem of widespread interference from radio sources right here on Earth.

Astronomer Jill Tarter is the director of the Institute for SETI Research in California. Tarter is often likened to the main character in the movie *Contact*. She heads a project called the Allen Telescope Array. It is named after Paul Allen, a businessman who donated money to help start the project. When completed, there will be about 350 separate radio receivers, each a little more than 20 feet (6 m) across. The total collecting area will rival the world's largest radio telescopes. Best of all, the total price is a fraction of what a single large dish would cost to build and maintain, so more money can be devoted to analyzing all the data.

Searching for extraterrestrial intelligence is surely the biggest gamble in science. No one knows if life exists anywhere else except Earth, but it would be a tremendous discovery to find it. The best thing about the search is that it will be rewarding even if it is never successful, because of the technological improvements and scientific data that will surely come from it.

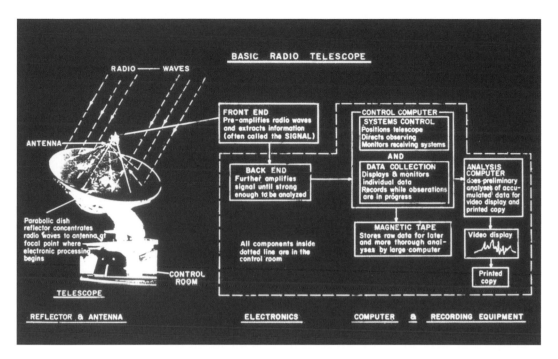

The set-up of a typical radio telescope. Rather than receiving optical images, it receives radio signals that are naturally emitted by stars.

SETI @ Home

Anyone with a home computer connected to the Internet can now participate in a radio SETI project. Data from the Arecibo dish, and other radio telescopes, is carved up into convenient chunks by computers at the SETI Institute. Then the data is sent to individual computers around the world. On each computer, a program uses the spare time in the computer's processing chips to analyze the parcel of data. The results are sent back over the Internet to the SETI Institute and coordinated there. Worldwide, more than four million people are participating. To join, go to www.setiathome.ssl.berkeley.edu.

GLOSSARY

amino acid One of the basic building blocks of life; chief component of proteins.

astronaut Person who travels beyond Earth's atmosphere.

bacteria Microscopic organisms with one-celled or noncellular bodies.

carbonates Chemical compounds.

cerebral cortex The outermost layer of the brain.

cosmic rays Streams of atomic nuclei that travel at great speed in space.

cyanobacteria Very simple life-forms.

deoxyribonucleic acid DNA, the carrier of genetic coding.

Drake Equation Mathematical formula to estimate the likelihood of intelligent aliens existing in our galaxy and in other galaxies.

extraterrestrials Beings originating or existing outside Earth and its atmosphere.

extremophile Any life-form that can live in conditions deadly to all other life-forms.

gigahertz Unit of frequency. It is equal to one billion hertz. A hertz is equal to one cycle per second.

glacier Enormous body of ice that moves very slowly.

greenhouse effect Warming of the Earth's surface and nearest layers of atmosphere.

helix Spiral in form.

hydrates Chemical compounds.

hydrogen bond Linkage of a hydrogen atom between two atoms of another element, such as oxygen.

hydrogen fusion Source of immense energy.

interstellar Located among the stars.

lightspeed 186,300 miles (300,000 km) per second.

metabolism Life process that provides and uses energy.

meteorite Meteor that reaches Earth's surface without being completely vaporized.

molecule Smallest particle of a substance that retains the properties of that substance and is made up of one or more atoms.

panspermia Theory that the building blocks of life arrived on Earth via meteorites and/or comets.

permafrost A permanently frozen layer lying below the Earth's surface.

planetesimals Huge rocks formed in the solar system from smaller rocks through the action of gravity and spinning motion.

plankton Tiny animal and plant life in the oceans.

polar molecule Molecule that is influenced slightly by electric charge.

polycyclic aromatic hydrocarbons Chemicals discovered in outer space by radio astronomers.

quinones Chemicals having ring-shaped molecules that resembles molecules found in living cells.

radioactivity Emissions by certain elements due to disintegration of the nuclei of atoms.

savannahs Subtropical or tropical grassland with few trees and drought-tolerant undergrowth.

silicon A nonmetallic element that can form four chemical bonds.

sulfates Chemical compounds.

INDEX